Don't Panic

Don't Panic

A book by South Africans, for South Africans

Alan Knott-Craig

PENGUIN BOOKS

PENGUIN BOOKS

Published By the Penguin Group
Penguin Books (South Africa) (Pty) Ltd, 24 Sturdee Avenue, Rosebank, Johannesburg 2196, South Africa
Penguin Books Ltd, 80 Strand, London WC2R 0RL, England
Penguin Group (USA) Inc, 375 Hudson Street, New York, New York 10014, USA
Penguin Group (Canada), 90 Eglinton Avenue East, Suite 700, Toronto, Ontario, M4P 2Y3, Canada (a division of Pearson Penguin Canada Inc.)
Penguin Ireland, 25 St Stephen's Green, Dublin 2, Ireland (a division of Penguin Books Ltd)
Penguin Group (Australia), 250 Camberwell Road, Camberwell, Victoria 3124, Australia (a division of Pearson Australia Group Pty Ltd)
Penguin Books India Pvt Ltd, 11 Community Centre, Panchsheel Park, New Delhi – 110 017, India
Penguin Group (NZ), 67 Apollo Drive, Mairangi Bay, Auckland 1310, New Zealand (a division of Pearson New Zealand Ltd)

Penguin Books (South Africa) (Pty) Ltd, Registered Offices:
24 Sturdee Avenue, Rosebank, Johannesburg 2196, South Africa

www.penguinbooks.co.za

First published by Penguin Books (South Africa) (Pty) Ltd 2008

Copyright © Penguin Books and iBurst 2008

ISBN: 978-0-143-02579-5

Typeset by PieRat Design in 10/12.5 Palatino
Cover design: Boss Repro
Printed and bound by Interpak Books, Pietermaritzburg

Contents

Publisher's preface

This book developed at a time in South Africa when we all needed the positives about our great country to be brought into focus, a time when many of us found ourselves weighed down by overwhelming negative sentiment. Alan started the drive to remind us of why we shouldn't be despondent and then others all over the country picked up the call – via our blog, by email and a few by SMS. This book provides a window on how South Africans are thinking about our country's challenges in 2008. We've included some headlines from newspapers of the last few decades to remind you that we have faced challenges before and have overcome them.

Many people who have contributed to the book have asked us to stop complaining and make sure that we put our personal effort into continuing South Africa's transformation process. We have included a few website addresses at the back of the book that point people towards positive stories about South Africa and ways you can get involved in making our country a better place. We will be adding to the list on our websites – visit

www.iburst.co.za and **www.penguinbooks.co.za** for updates to this list.

Louise Grantham, Publisher

Acknowledgements

Thank you to the following people for making this book a reality:

Callia Doucas, Nicole Menego and Mark Hartley from iBurst.
Ivan Booth from Reliable Sources.
Mondli Makhanya, Michelle Leon and Pat Geddie from Sunday Times.
Nazeer Howa, Simone Deyzel and Angela Lotter from Independent Newspapers.
Louise Grantham from Penguin Books.
Warren Goldstein
David Bullard
Andile Ngcaba
Sam Cowen
Noeleen Maholwana-Sangqu
John Robbie
Martine Schaffer
Kim Feinberg
Branko Brkic

Introduction

Picture it: the summer of 2008, an overcast Joburg day. There I was minding my own business, when suddenly my office is full of coffee and I am swamped with letters and phone calls! An innocent memo to the iBurst staff triggered quite an amazing response, and made me realize that many people just need a nudge to get some perspective in the midst of the sudden negativity that swept in with 2008.

Hence this book.

We have compiled a selection of opinions from a wide-ranging group of people, both well-known and unknown, with the intention of showing the perspective of others.

The intention is not to paint a perfect picture and sugar-coat the very real and serious problems we have. It's not great to deal with Joburg traffic at 8am during load-shedding. Shatter-proof windows are not so much needed as protection against would-be hijackers, but rather as a shield against road-ragers!

The reaction to my infamous email led me to the conclusion that not everyone is able to put things in perspective, and that many people are being carried away on the tsunami of negativity.

Will we still have a viable country in 2020? I think we've got a better than 50/50 chance, otherwise I wouldn't be here. Is it a slam-dunk? Hell no. Crime, service delivery and education are just some of the problems that need to be addressed; otherwise we're dead in the water. But it's still an absolutely terrific country to live in if you're striving to get ahead in life.

So I guess the aim of this book is to help you sit back, look at the positives and the negatives about sunny SA, and choose your direction regardless of what everyone else is doing.

Alan Knott-Craig, iBurst MD, Johannesburg
April 2008

The email that started it all ...

MD's message - What a start to 2008...

2008 has certainly started with a bang! The future was rosy on 31 December 2007, but suddenly everyone is buying candles and researching property in Perth! A combination of recession in the USA, global equity market negativity, high interest rates, the National Credit Act and power outages have combined to create the perfect storm.

But don't panic!

This is not the first time there's been doom and gloom. Every few years the same thing happens. We experience massive economic growth, everyone is optimistic and buying Nescafé Gold, and holiday homes and Mercs. The positivity gets ahead of itself and the economy overheats, and then panic sets in because the economy seems to be collapsing when in actual fact it's simply making an adjustment back to a reasonable level.

It happened in 1989, when SA defaulted on its international loans and the stock market and Rand crashed, it happened in 1994 when the ANC took power and everyone thought war would break out, it happened in 1998 when interest rates hit 25% and you couldn't give away your house, and it happened in 2001 when a fairly unstable guy by the name of Osama arranged for 2 Boeings to fly into the tallest buildings in New York!

On each of those occasions everyone thought it was the end of the world and that there was no light in sight. And on each occasion, believe it or not, the world did not actually end, it recovered and in fact things continued to get better.

I think 2008 will be a tough year, but I also see it as a great opportunity to seize the day whilst everyone else is whinging and get a front seat on the inevitable boom that we'll experience in 2009, 2010 and beyond.

Make sure you make a mental note of everything that is happening now, because it will happen again and again, and if you don't recognise the symptoms you'll be suckered into the same negativity, and forget to look for the opportunities.

It's easy to be negative. Subconsciously, you WANT to be negative! Whenever you open the papers they tell you about the goriest hijacking and the most corrupt politicians. Why don't they dedicate more pages to the fact that Joburg is the world's biggest man-made forest, or to the corruption-free achievements of the vast majority of public officials? Because bad news sells. Good news is boring.

SA still has the best weather in world! We're lucky enough to possess a huge chunk of the world's resources, i.e.: gold, platinum, coal, iron. The growth in India and China will continue to accelerate (India and China sign 10 million new mobile customers every month), and so will their demand for our resources. The government has already embarked on massive infrastructure projects (some of them a tad late, i.e.: electricity), and this will pump money into the economy.

We are all lucky enough to be a part of the birth of a massive and all-encompassing industry. The Internet has and will continue to change the world. The enormity of its impact is up there with the wheel, electricity, TV, telephones, and possibly man's greatest ever invention, coffee. Not only does it open up an entirely untapped world of commerce, but it is also the ultimate disseminator of information and news. Apartheid would not have lasted 40 years if the Internet had existed! And you're part of it!

I'm looking forward to another year of ASA complaints, IR issues, Plug & Wireless parties, BTS roll-outs, billing runs, irate customers, happy customers, orange bubbles, faulty elevators, etc, etc. The nice stuff makes me feel good, and the challenges remind me why we can beat the competition. Most importantly, I'm looking forward to having fun and making memories.

So ignore the doomsayers, install a timer on your geyser, and buy Ricoffee for a couple of months.

Alan

CONTRIBUTIONS FROM
SOUTH AFRICA

No one knows enough to be a pessimist

It is understandable, after a long and agonising journey, that those who've emigrated justify their decision vociferously. It is a huge wrench, the reality of which can never be anticipated and hence the need to continually remind oneself, and anyone who cares to listen, of the precipitating and maintaining factors.

Behind closed doors, I hear different stories. One grandmother stated: 'You know, it's the little things, what happened at school today? How did the doctor's appointment go? And the details of daily life that fill conversation and serve as connecting glue when living nearby. The little things, the minutiae, are really the big things. It is impossible, however sophisticated technology might be, to develop and maintain a remotely similar involvement long distance. Sure, we speak all the time but it is still long distance.'

What is often not realised is the process supersedes the content. It's not what you say but that you are talking which confirms and develops connection. Most people refer to quality of relationship and look forward to the next occasion, holiday or visit. However, we need quantity to build quality. It's a challenge to have three weeks of quality time at the end of the year with minimal quantity for the rest. The family life cycle is like a river ... forever flowing. If you miss the moment you've missed it. Sure there are others, but not that one.

One father who emigrated and returned with his family said: 'We left because of the crime and yes, maybe returned to the crime ... but you know what, the price was just too high. We are living an amazing life here celebrating and valuing the support and connection every day. My children love their school and have grandparents who are an integral part of their lives. We now know there is no substitute for that.'

A business woman now living in London states: 'I am an invisible, anonymous person. I have to start from the beginning – just a number in a queue. There is no family history, credit rating, GP or greengrocer. It's hard to start all over again.'

Most people underestimate the importance of 'transcendental connectedness', a sense of past which is woven into the fabric of your being, affects the present and enriches the future. They make new friends but miss 'remember when'. There is an attraction and resonance with fellow South Africans because of the innate human need for belonging and community. New relationships develop, but these are not coloured or energised by history and tend to be mostly social and activity-orientated.

So what to do? Physical safety and survival is the most basic of human needs. After that on Maslow's hierarchy comes the need for belonging.

There are very real issues affecting all of our lives in our wonderful country but the choice of response is a personal one, although largely determined by those around us. Feelings and attitudes are more contagious than any virus and we get caught up in a heartbeat in a pervasive sense of panic or indeed euphoria, as we did just after the '94 election.

The fact is, as you think so shall you be. If we are cynical, hopeless and pessimistic we unconsciously select evidence to continually confirm our position. This dominates our minds, our hearts and our conversation, and will be felt at a visceral level, even if unexpressed by those around us. This communication is deep and subtle, almost like birds flying in a flock and suddenly changing direction without instruction.

When the lights went out, coupled with a series of senseless and devastating murders, the downturn of the economy and pervasive political uncertainty, we reached the pro-verbial 'tipping point'. All the potholes grew bigger overnight, fears of sewerage spilling into the street, political anarchy and recession prevailed, and above all, insecurity and anxiety concerning our safety and that of our children was rife and overflowing. Two months later there is still a huge concern but a somewhat calmer perspective. *'Life is not a matter of holding good cards but of playing a poor hand well,'* said Robert Louis Stevenson.

So what are the different responses?

- The Fatalist - 'what will be will be', characterised by the belief that fate and destiny reign supreme and cannot be influenced.
- The Denier - the ostrich mentality. The hope is that by burying one's head in the sand and restricting your world, maybe all of this will disappear in the morning.
- The Pessimist – characterised by binocular vision. The bad is magnified and overwhelming to the point where anything positive is minimised and reframed negatively.
- The Realist – an attempt to be well informed and offer hardcore facts but often uses the present or the past to predict the future and thus finds it difficult to imagine a different scenario.
- The Unbridled Optimist – finds it difficult to focus on current negative realities and will tend to dismiss glaring facts by saying, 'we've been here before and we'll get out of it again'. There is an attempt to placate the pessimist and the realist by continually pointing out that other countries have worse problems and bad weather.
- The Cautious Optimist - understands present realities, is well informed and strongly believes that commitment and focused

intervention can make a difference. They tend to be life participants and influencers of others. They know that thoughts create actions and actions create results and thereby believe that destiny can, to a large extent, be modified. They recognise the inherent goodwill of the vast majority of all of our people and help develop a strategy to mobilise, energise, focus and manifest a common desired outcome. They seldom give up. They are mindful and honouring of others while also listening to their own inner drumbeat. True leaders, they are connectors, authentic and inspiring. They make things happen. Fortunately there are many such South Africans and as Trevor Manuel said many times in his budget speech, 'we are all in this together'.

In his poem 'If', Rudyard Kipling refers to many dimensions of maturity and it would serve us well to remember his words *'If you can keep your head when all about you are losing theirs ... Yours is the Earth and everything that's in it, and - which is more - you'll be a Man, my son!'*

Dorianne Weil, Clinical Psychologist 'Dr D,'

Tomorrow Trust Trustee

1991

Sunday Times

Top prisons brass named as targets for gifts and cash by company

GENERALS IN BRIBES PROBE

2003

THE SUNDAY INDEPENDENT

Boks into the last-chance saloon

November 21 2004 / R. INC S. VAT

2004

Good times roll for SA

People's optimism soars as economy powers ahead in longest boom since war

2003

johnnic

Sunday Times

THE PAPER FOR THE PEOPLE

www.sundaytimes.co.za

Zuma off the hook

Scorpions have evidence of corruption, but it's 'not strong enough'

2002

www.sundaytimes.co.za

johnnic

Sunday Times

COMPLIMENTARY: GLOBAL VILLAGE MARKET

Bumper festive season for SA

...nd, spend, spend

Tourism up in 'sexy' destination and...

MAY 9 2004

johnnic

Sunday Times

THE PAPER FOR THE PEOPLE

www.sundaytimes.co.za

AFRICA

Big boom in SA's super-rich

Wealth explosion brings more than 500 newcomers into the ultra-elite in 10 years

2007

SUNDAY SPORT

Boks rule the world!

Returning home

I was living in the UK from 2001 to 2007. I returned home late November 2007, to be greeted with the best welcome one could ever have. My daughter has blossomed into an outdoor person and loves life here, she had had more dirty feet in two weeks of being home than in 5 years of her life in England.

Many people ask me why I did return, I have one answer, 'there is no place like home'. I love being back and have taken this opportunity and embraced it, I found a great job within 3 days of being back and love it! My husband and I are happy with our decision and want to say: 'Stop running - the grass is not greener on the other side.'

SA has its problems but so do many other places. The UK - huge problems with gangs, knife-crime, youths, the list is endless. Australia - Sydney has a huge problem with drugs, knife-crime, so why are you running from place to place?

Stay home ... it's the best place in the world.

Claudia Gomes, Johannesburg

Thanks for making my day

To the MD of iBurst ... well it's about time that people understood that there is always good news around the corner and your email was truly uplifting. Many thanks for making my day.

Zahir, Kinshasa

The four-way stop phenomenon

Two wrongs hardly ever make a right, except in places where right and wrong are so inextricably entwined that they become virtually indistinguishable. Johannesburg is such a place. Two of the city's lesser evils are traffic and power failures. Having respectively threatened me with loss of life (sudden death) and loss of text (sudden PC shutdown) for several days, this duo conspired to restore my faith in humanity.

How, you may well ask?

The four-way stop, I would answer. To the best of my knowledge, this is a uniquely South African phenomenon, which owes its success to a deep-seated sense of social responsibility and celebrates our universal desire for justice and equality, embodied by that truly humane and logical principle: 'First come, first served.' After a power failure dimmed the traffic lights at a busy intersection, I was amazed to see all the metal-clad psychopaths – taxis, SUVs, 18-

wheelers, bakkies and mid-priced sedans - gear back and offer their fellow motorists right of way, with nary a hoot nor raised finger. Calmly they waited their turn, making eye contact, waving each other through, subdued and united in their common fate. Give it some thought the next time you encounter the simple humanity of the four-way stop.

Richard de Nooy

So much to be proud of

We keep comparing ourselves to Australia, Canada, the UK and the USA. These are all developed countries. We are a developing country, and it's impossible to measure up to the advancements that the developed world has on offer. We have so much to be proud of in the short time that we have become an inclusive democracy. The fact is there has been little bloodshed over our major political transition, more people are getting housing and services, our constitution is the most advanced in the world and our economy has performed against all odds. It's time to recognise the great achievements that are being made in our country each and every day. There is a reason that South Africa is loved by the rest of the world - and it's not just the sunshine.

Martine Schaffer, Homecoming Revolution

Tough times

I agree, times are getting tough. A string of perfect storms is hitting these southern skies and it is nigh impossible not to be affected by their poisoned air. The doomsayers shout that this country is finally paying the price for centuries of mismanagement and politically correct blindness. Maybe the highest price of all will be a loss of hope that 'things will get better'. That hope certainly seems to be evading us right now.

It can be tempting in times like these to give up, to surrender to creeping entropy. There is, after all, a certain measure of comfort in surrender. The peverse need to give up grows as the adversity you're facing reaches greater and greater heights – to give up your value system, your dreams and hopes, your ideas for a better world; to give up the fight to be better every day, for the rest of your life.

The adversity you're facing draws its awesome power from stupidity and ugliness; it's corrupt to its core and will not rest until it sees you on your knees, part of the process, defeated at a very fundamental level. It wants to see you humiliated, impoverished, accepting of its warped morals and pseudo-intellectual constructs.

Yes, faced with odds as big as these, the average citizen of a troubled South Africa in late summer '08 is sorely tempted to give up.

Or worse, just leave.

But that is an average citizen I'm talking about. Not you. You're a maverick. Giving up is not an option, here or anywhere, any time. You know who you are, and you know what you value in life. You understand that selling your principles is a sacrifice that will leave you scarred for the rest of you life, a price that is too much to pay for a human being of your integrity and brains.

Think about this when entropy starts banging at the gates of your being. Your uniqueness is an affront to it; your clear thought unbearable to the force of chaos, your system of values an antidote to its corrosiveness. Deep within you remains your greatest treasure: your restless, ever-wandering soul. No matter how difficult the times, the true maverick's soul will never be for sale. At any price.

Branko Brkic, *Maverick* Magazine
(editorial March 2008)

Wisdom from my son

One of the most incredible aspects of being a woman – no matter what your country of birth - is being a mother. It is not a job, but in some way it is. You may not be paid a salary at the end of the month, but you sure do get many rewards. One of the many rewards of being a mother is the teachings about patience, tolerance and recently for me - perspective.

Here I am, a 40-year-old South African woman, worried about my country. I would have to be incredibly stupid and naïve not to be worried. Violent crime. Everyone knows someone who has been hit. Poverty. Look around any of the big cities, smaller towns and rural areas. South Africans are hungry. The never-ending increase in the petrol price, the rand against major currencies, the inflation rate on the up. Everything seems to be in disarray. It is confusing; it is upsetting.

So when things are bad you tend to vocalise it. You harp on the problems. When things are bad, it is only human nature to throw your hands up in the air and give up in despair.

That is until my 13-year-old son made a comment, or rather, asked me a question typical of a 13-year-old who is going on 20. His question was why is it that every time you land at OR Tambo International Airport you say: 'It is great to be home, there is no place like South Africa'?

That is true. That is what I say. He then asked me why I do not practise what I preach. He reminded me that every time he has a problem I usually say - 'don't tell me about the problems - give me the solutions'. What he was basically saying is that no matter how hard, how tough - I still love South Africa.

What this 13-year-old boy was reminding me was, that if you love something you don't throw it out with the bath water. What he was saying was – find solutions.

I can't stabilise the rand, I can't decrease the oil price. However, there are things that I can do. I can help by not throwing up my hands in the air. I can help by creating jobs. I can help by changing my lifestyle. I can save electricity. I can help in so many ways. If all of us can start with a small step, just lending a hand to one person, changing our attitudes to a lot of things, I think we can go a long way.

Noeleen Maholwana-Sangqu,
3Talk host

The South African dream!

... we can definitely make a difference in our lives and to those close to us. South Africa abounds with opportunities, no doubt about it! However only those with positive attitudes will be in a position to seize them and fly! Come on guys! We have the best IT infrastructure, roads, world-class business schools, companies and leaders – that's the dream I'm talking about! Why should it always sound better when South African is replaced by American? Why should we even consider

Perth? There is a lot that we can achieve as a collective in South Africa, we can all make meaningful contributions towards nation-building (by a collective I refer to whites, blacks, Indians, etc.)

In conclusion, I would like to quote a trailblazer of black business, CEO of Pamodzi Investment Holdings and Ernst and Young World Best Entrepreneur for South Africa, Ndaba Ntsele: 'Hard work goes hand in hand with a positive attitude, it's a precursor for good things to happen in life. You create them because you dream about them. You create your life through being positive and having integrity. If there is suffering and negativity, come up with positive ideas to alleviate them. Positivity creates wealth, so we have to create a culture of positivity in South Africa.'

Mbuyiselo Xaba

Why SA is still the best place

I think my husband must be one of the most patriotic South Africans. Even though he has been hijacked twice (in one incident the gun was held to his head and the trigger jammed), he still has a positive attitude about this country and defends it to the last.

We still have the cheapest petrol (even

though it is now over R8.00/litre).

We have a brilliant climate and good weather most of the year round.

We have managed to overcome most of the apartheid issues with less trouble than was expected, we elected a president of colour before America did and they always proclaim to be the first in most situations.

Because we are still a relatively young country and still growing, there are so many business opportunities available. I love living here and shudder every time I think of those poor people living in England – we are very fortunate to have the space available to us to enjoy our home environment. We are the hub of Africa. Here's to many more days of biltong, *boerewors*, *braaivleis*, sunny skies and rugby.

Kim Laing, Midrand

Why I like SA

Developed countries are, simply put, boring. I'd never live in a country where there is more chance of you killing yourself than someone else killing you.

South Africa is full of opportunity. Where the greatest dangers lurk, also lurk the greatest opportunities. Power outages? An

Sunday Times
THE PAPER FOR THE PEOPLE

1996

Mandela in move to end panic over rand

Sunday Times

2006

Scramble to avert national power collapse

Eskom goes into panic mode as South Africa runs out of electricity with winter only months away

BUSINESSDAY

Tuesday, February 1 2005

Printed in Johannesburg, Cape Town and Durban

www.businessday.co.za

2005

Sunday Times

2003

THE PAPER FOR THE PEOPLE

www.sundaytimes.co.za

Spending spree powers economy

Consumers fuel a boom that's expected to last for six months

Consumer credit at 7-year high clouds outlook for rate cut

Sunday Times

End of censorship

Sunday Times

2000

THE PAPER FOR THE PEOPLE   www.sundaytimes.co.za

YOUR LOTTERY PAPER: Official Lotto coupon in the Magazine

7 12 16 28 35 41 ✚ 30

WIN R20 0... CASH TODA...

World Cup coup

Soccer supremo Blatter in secret talks to snatch first-round victory for S...

opportunity to build generators. Primal chaos? Opportunities to make money in general and to have one's self amused free of charge.

In the UK, for example, it's all been done before. There are 100 people doing every niche thing and chances are they're smarter than you and doing it better than you could ever do it. I like things a little easier. Plus I like warm weather.

When someone from abroad asks you what SA is like, please reply as follows:

'It's terrible – never go there.'

Then we can keep this God-given place all to ourselves.

Jonathan Hoch, Johannesburg

The most beautiful country in the world

We are lucky enough to live in one of the most beautiful countries in the world. We enjoy the coast, the Karoo, the mountains and the city; what more could you ask for? Beautiful weather, friendly people and a great standard of living? You've got it. Sure there is crime, poverty and sadness, it's everywhere. We keep trying to make a difference and counting ourselves lucky that we have what we do for as long as we can make it last.

Ann Baker, Johannesburg

We hold the answer

The saddest thing about South Africa today is that old pigeonholes still exist as bolt-holes. Think about it. The philosophy of the past was that people could be forced into boxes based on the colour of their skin. Most people realised or came to realise that this system was both unworkable and deeply wrong. You can't generalise about people based on skin colour no more than you can based on hair colour or the colour of eyes or whether they choose to open their boiled breakfast eggs at the pointy or flat end. Jonathan Swift used this example to capture the stupidity of racism and tribalism in *Gulliver's Travels*.

Thank God people realised this and the Rainbow Nation was born and bought into spiritually and emotionally by the vast majority of people. Think back to 1990, to 1994, to the first Rugby World Cup win and the victory in the soccer African Cup of Nations? That was about real South Africans, you and me, one flag, one nation. Look at France last year! That spirit still exists here, as long as things go well. This is the nub of the issue. Why doesn't it shine through at all times?

It was naïve to think that all South African problems would simply disappear with the advent of democracy. For those with jobs, houses and health, the level of violent crime is the number one concern at the moment. I know it is for me and my family, and like most people, we have been directly affected. The fight against crime is a war to be won. It is a just war and such conflicts should be embraced by all of us, body and soul. The saddest thing is that instead of this fight being a unifying thing it is divisive, as with so many issues here. Suddenly people feel it's 'us' and 'them'. Dreadful crimes are emotionally pigeonholed. Who is the victim? Who is the perpetrator? Is the crime across a colour line? Is the suspect a foreigner or South African? Is the victim wealthy or from a squatter camp? Tragically, the level or nature of our response is affected by such questions. Can you believe it?

People are talking about protest marches instead of getting involved in the fight. When Churchill called on the British to fight them on the beaches, did the population stage an protest march against Hitler? Not on your life. Those who weren't in the frontline already, were soon digging for victory, working in munitions factories or down the mines or risking their lives on the North Atlantic convoys. The war brought all people together and their united action won through.

Sadly, here, when there is insecurity and fear, people start to distrust their emotions concerning unity and retreat to the nonsense of the past. *Swart gevaar*, allegations of racial superiority, belief in secret agendas, third forces, all of these nation killers reappear when people are scared. Even the AWB are threatening to get back on their horses and ride again after ET went home years ago.

Perhaps the combination of political shenanigans in the ruling party, festering fears about corruption, the Eskom situation, crime levels and maybe even the Pandora's box opened in Kenya, have fuelled the negativity. Lack of real leadership concerning these issues is certainly a major factor in them gaining currency. However, that spirit of unity still exists as well; the spirit that prevented this country going the way of Iraq or Burundi. It is there in the vast majority of people you meet in everyday life. People are scared, but not cowards. Bravery is acting to overcome fear. The question is: how do we harness this spirit to fight the scourge of crime and all the other problems we face? Together. Achieve that and nothing is impossible in South Africa. I don't have the answer but I know it starts inside each of us.

John Robbie, Radio 702

A big shout-out to South Africa!

It is shortly before seven pm, the time when every channel broadcasts bad news into the world, from the petrol price to renewed load-shedding, it seems bad news will never stop. Then suddenly I feel the cool air arriving over the mountain after another blistering hot day in Cape Town, and I notice some guinea fowl foraging in my garden next to the nature reserve. Wow, what a beautiful country we live in!

It is about then I read about the captain's letter to the staff at iBurst, and I think, what we all need is a letter like this from our country's captain, Mr Mbeki, encouraging every South African not to panic, and to fight for this beautiful country we live in by working together and achieving success together.

Long enough we have all been like ostriches, burying our heads in the sand, pretending nothing can be done whilst hoping things will eventually get better. The fact is, if we do stand together, work together and respect each other, this country will regain its 'shine' quicker and we won't have to wait that long before the proverbial financial sun will shine again.

So if you're the captain of your company, business team or family, sit down take note of the good things around you, forget for a second about those bad thoughts, don't watch the seven o'clock news, and raise a glass to South Africa and praise everybody in your circle that makes this country the best place in the world.

Mornay Walters

Proud to be South African

Whenever I see or hear people of different races laughing and joking together I feel so proud to be South African and I am reminded of how far we have come!

Michelle Taylor

There is no need to panic

In 1994 all the world, the gloomers and doomers, thought SA was going the same way as the rest of Africa and it did not - we are not alone.

In 2008 the same disease is emerging from many corners and they still think SA will go the same way and this will not happen - we are not alone.

In all of humanity we have the inherent gift of hope and in SA we need to nurture this and spread it around. There is hope - we are not alone.

In 1993 blessed Mother Theresa was approached by those who saw gloom and doom to ask what she would recommend for SA. She said pray, pray, pray - we are not alone.

So in 2008 we need not panic, all we have to do is resolve our issues as a united rainbow nation, have hope and be resilient. History has proved this and - we are not alone. So why the panic?

Marco

I'm back and proudly South African!

I had of course heard about the crime in South Africa. Who hasn't?

After nearly six years in London, I am here now. I do not wish to be obvious and I do not wish to be overly simplistic in my reasons for returning from Britain. It is always so dull. I also don't want to sound anything but totally in love with my country; passionate and utterly idealistic.

Let's try for a moment to look at some of the real reasons people like us should be coming back. Let's get this straight up . . . if the only reasons we come back are Mrs Balls, friends and family, the weather, the Boks, Rajah Curry Powder or Nik Naks then it won't be long before we are craving a warm pint or an annoying drawl. The satisfaction of our first fresh Tex Bar or that slug of Castle next to the sizzling *wors* is very quickly forgotten as the realities of crime, load-shedding, soaring interest rates, dodgy politics, traffic and massive inflation set in.

So why am I so chuffed to be back? Why, when faced with all the challenges, do I love it more than ever? Is it just because I've only been back for a year? I keep thinking that I'll wake up tomorrow and the light will have gone out (sorry!). It doesn't.

The thing for me is this: our waking thoughts have to change. Our attitude has to change.

Our mindset needs to change. We mustn't come back (or consider coming back) in spite of the problems, we must come back because of them. We must quit seeking a better life and start seeking ways in which we can make life better.

Our reality is a truly miraculous one ... very few countries that we would flee to present us with the opportunities South Africa does. In our lifetime we have seen the demise of one of the cruellest regimes in history. We all seem to forget what a massive achievement that was and it's really not very long ago at all. Do we honestly believe that a nation that brought apartheid to its knees can't beat crime? For heaven's sake, the criminal sewer called New York managed to reduce violent crime by 62% in just 5 years - and let's be honest - they haven't dismantled apartheid properly yet (viva Obama viva!).

Have we got so jaded, so cynical, that we really believe that load-shedding is an insurmountable problem ... a problem to leave the country over or not return because of? All we have to do is cut our usage by 20% ... is that it? Is that the extent of the problem that is currently bringing our economy to its knees? Driving up inflation? Weakening the rand?

Let's stop looking to the government or big business to sort out the problems. Screw it ... let's do it ourselves. Let's say to the world that yes, we have massive problems, but we respect one another and our heritage too much to carry on moaning and not to roll up our sleeves and get stuck in.

Let's get out there and start by actively respecting and dignifying one another. I mean really. Let's get rid of negative language or even the indifference of silence and replace it with a humanising, '*ubuntu*-ising' attitude. Greet one another and smile. Be courteous. Be thankful. Be fair.

You may be surprised to hear this, but these simple attitude shifts and daily practices have been proven to combat crime. We tend to think that in order to make a difference we need to do something big and 'impressive'. Not so. We don't actually need to become a police reservist (unless we wish to), or start a block watch (unless we wish to) or give loads of money and time (unless we wish to). Big change is brought about by small actions repeated often.

Justin Foxton

I love South Africa

Why do I love South Africa? There are so many reasons . . .

Table Mountain, fynbos, biltong and Afrikaans are all unique parts of our beautiful country, South Africa.

We South Africans are sports-mad with brilliant sports teams ... well some of them. Our cricket team is one of the best in the world, but I can't say the same about the soccer team ...

Along with our brilliant sporting ability comes a great sense of humour. If you go to the cricket at Newlands, you're most likely to hear the ice-cream men shouting, 'Lolly, lolly, *lekker* lolly, iiccee-crrrim!' or ' '*n* Sucker *maak jou wakker*, a lolly *maak jou* jolly!' Then you'd hear the guy sitting behind you screaming, 'Smith, my granny can bat better than you!!'

Another 'special' aspect of South Africa is the minibus taxi driver. They hoot, push in and stop in the middle of the road, but you'd miss them if you emigrated, guaranteed. Their taxis usually have tiny white wall tyres, plastic spinners and some huge sticker of a wolf on the back window.

Even our health minister is special, always remember, eating lots of vegetables will cure AIDS!

And as for food ... there's nothing better than creamy milk tart, sweet, crispy *koeksusters*, *pap* and *wors*, spicy biltong and steak sizzling on a braai.

Then there are the languages ... South Africa has 11 official languages! South African English could be considered a whole new language by tourists. Just imagine you lived overseas and you heard this conversation:

'Hey bru, that chorb on your chin looks mif, it's gonna make the chix *skrik* man!'

'Hey, I'll *klap* you man! Jislaaik, I know hey, this chorb is hectic! I'm so *gatvol* with these flippen zits!'

'Shame man, lets go get sum of that zit zapper stuff that I saw on TV!'

After listening to me, how could you not say, 'I love South Africa!'

Stewart Steenkamp (age 12)

South Africa's treasure

Our people are our greatest treasure here in South Africa. We are indeed a nation of heroes. We will never forget that as we stood in long queues in 1994 to vote in our first democratic elections, we felt inspired and uplifted by the greatness of the South African spirit. Millions of people across the length and breadth of this land are great human beings who go about their lives with courage and tenacity as they battle against enormous adversity. They live with dedication and commitment to earning an honest living, raising their children and trying to give them better life and opportunities. Our future must be based on an appreciation and respect for every human being. We need to demand from those who have been elected to serve us that we be served with compassion, that we not be treated as statistics but rather as people of unlimited value and preciousness. We deserve nothing less; South Africans have suffered for too long.

We need to live with a respect and appreciation of the awesome power of the human spirit. It is our moral calling to create a society in which the human spirit can flourish. The enterprise of building a great South Africa is about ensuring that the conditions for nurturing great people are in place. Apartheid tried to destroy the human spirit. 'Nasty, brutish and short', are the famous words of Thomas Hobbes to describe life in the state of nature without human civilisation. They are also accurate words to describe life in the old South Africa. The sacred enterprise of building human civilisation in the new South Africa is about creating spaces within which the human spirit can achieve its greatness. This is true on a physical, social and moral level.

All of this is about the Talmudic principle 'Tikkun Olam', which literally means to fix the world. The world, we are taught, is in a state of disrepair, and is filled with human suffering, and it is our sacred duty to repair and heal it. In South Africa, as we strive to overcome the devastation of apartheid, Tikkun Olam is our mission. South Africans

are not strangers to adversity. We have in
our past overcome obstacles which seemed
insurmountable. The Book of Proverbs says:
'G-d will wipe away tears from off all faces'.
The beloved country has cried for too long. Let
us join hands to build a truly great country
and wipe away her tears of suffering. Let us
resolve to overcome our current challenges
too and to become stronger from them, let our
sorrow become the seed of our salvation, as
the Book of Psalms says: 'May those who sowed
in tears, reap in joy.'

Rabbi Warren Goldstein,
Chief Rabbi, South Africa

Think right

There is something that everyone in South
Africa (and the world) can do to help.

The universe thinks that what you are
thinking about is what you want, and lovingly
gives you more of the same.

If your mind is full of murder and mayhem,
you will create more. All that is needed is
to concentrate on peace and brotherhood, or
if this is too difficult, imagine a healing
golden light covering our land. Our thoughts
will go out like beams from a lighthouse and
combine in a rolling mass that can bring about
positive change and stability.

It will not cost you anything, and you can practise it anywhere.

Stella Ann Rigby

SA is the best!

My family and I have been living in the UK for the past 10 years but after a holiday in SA this February, we all decided not to stay in the UK for one day longer than necessary. We have always known that we will return one day but that day is most definitely going to be much sooner than anticipated. My youngest still has to complete her schooling (another 1½ years) but she is excited at the possibility of attending a South African university.

Most of the moaners in SA think that the grass is greener on the other side because they do not have anything to compare it with. Well, don't think everything is so rosy this side! For starters, the weather is totally sh*t, houses are so small you can't swing a cat in them and worst of all, the UK is a total police state. There is no freedom here as every aspect of your life is ruled by ridiculous laws and regulations because of the compensation culture that is rife in the UK. Because of this there is no such thing as initiative or common sense. Criminals here have more rights than the victim and you don't even try to defend yourself against an attacker! You will be the one who lands up in jail. Also don't think that you don't ever land up banging your head against a wall because of the incompetence of officials over here... Yes, crime is a problem in SA but don't think this place is crime free and of course over here we have the extra fear of the suicide bomber on the underground!

So, enjoy the most fantastic country in the world, be positive and help to build a vibrant new nation and culture. Seek the good in things instead of depressing yourself with negatives. Enjoy the biltong, braai and snoek on the coals, the friendly people, hot summer holidays at the beach; *ag* man, I *sommer* want to cry! I am jealous of the fact that you are there and I am here but I am working hard on it to return a.s.a.p. See you soon...

Johann and family

Positive thoughts

Something I saw that lifted my heart (allow me to mention race): outside a nursery in Hermanus three sales ladies - one white, one black, one coloured - were huddled together in the sun. They had a big stick of biltong and a huge knife that they were passing to each other, cutting off thick slices of the meat and giggling as they chewed.

It made me feel so good and so positive.

Especially in the light of the terrible episode at the student hostel in the Free State.

Barbara Swart, Hermanus

South Africa

We were attacked by four men at our home in 2004. My husband was shot and passed away later in hospital. I moved off the property during the day and went to live with my parents. Ten days later we were attacked again by four men at my parents' home. This time my daughter and her friend were held at gunpoint but thankfully there were no fatalities.

In January 2005 I encountered a smash 'n grab at an intersection; my handbag was taken. I encountered another smash 'n grab incident later that year.

Elaborating on the details of each incident is not for this forum, but to say that I still believe this country has so much potential and instead of running away, or complaining, we, as South Africans, should stand together and do something about what is happening. My desire has been for the bad that has happened to turn into good. Through Esther's obedience, commitment and dedication, she saved a nation from destruction - Israel. Change can start with one person!

I do not have all the answers but I vote

against anything that I believe to be morally incorrect or detrimental to our nation or its people. I also encourage others to do the same. I voice my opinion regarding articles printed in the media where I believe comment to be relevant. I write to the metropolitan councils relating to issues of health, cleanliness, road works, etc. This includes television networks that air undesirable programmes – especially detrimental to children. I believe we also need proper voter education.

Don't you think that if we got more involved we would feel better about ourselves as well as our country? This country can be the 'light to the rest of the world' if we will do our part.

Linky de Jongh-Brown

Tolerance

Tolerance doesn't mean taking people or things as they are but instead embracing people with their faults and always looking for the positive in them. This is what SA is about. We understand our differences and the baggage that every race comes with, but still embrace everyone with dignity and love. We are not saying people should forget, rather forgive and move on, understanding that we all have been dragged into this misfortune (apartheid). It is up to each and every South African to change the past and views of other countries and show them that we are a tolerant country and we all want to be part of a free and peaceful nation for generations to come. *Phambili Mzantsi phambili* all eyes are on you!

Busisiwe Mbiyo

The right perspective

It's all about the right perspective. Have you lived abroad long enough to miss home? My husband and I lived in the UK for 6 years and returned to SA in 2004, realising that there truly is no place like home. When you live abroad, you never truly feel like you belong or fit in with that country's culture.

The two biggest reasons (among many others) for returning to SA were: family/friends and schooling. The bond that South African families share is a very strong one and raising children without the closeness of grandparents, aunties, uncles, cousins, etc. is very lonely.

Other reasons for returning to SA : fantastic entrepreneurial opportunities, wonderful weather, beautiful homes, green suburbs, ample 'green' space, good infrastructure - roads, water/electricity supply, telecommunications, foreign relations, good, affordable property investment, beautiful holiday destinations on your doorstep, wonderful traditions and culture, amazing sports people and national talent, friendliness and vibe, great private healthcare - the best doctors in the world, openness with regards to faith, a peaceful transition from white to black government in 1994, Nelson Mandela.

I could sit here and make the list longer but I have to work. Please think before you leave SA, our country needs you to help build our growing economy.

SJ

Right perspective – part two

I feel the need to comment on what my wife has written (above). I could not be prouder of being here in SA. My wife and I believe in and follow Christ in all that we do and are - as much as we possibly can. Sometimes we fail or fall miserably short of what is required of us as Christians - but that does not mean we are not Christians or that we don't love our God (and vice versa) ... it just means that we are human and we are trying. The same should be said for our great country ... yes it may seem that at the moment things are looking bleak and that the government is not keeping its end of the bargain in securing basic necessities (lights, water in rural areas, schooling, etc.) ... but as my point above states, it does not mean that it is giving up on us. We are a young country in the grand scheme of things and as much as it takes a village to raise a child so does it take dedication and pride on behalf of the population to raise a country out of its challenges. My wife and I will not speak negatively about our country or its people to our children, because we want them to believe that they are living in a great country and they can make a great difference when they are able to.

Justin

South Africa – a 'going concern'

Earlier this year, in the midst of all the 'rolling load-shedding' my wife and I went to a well-known Italian restaurant in Illovo, Johannesburg, in the company of other 'blacked-out' friends. The physical ambience was homely and warm; the pizza oven burned like a hearth in the background, small emergency lamps and candles cast an almost romantic hue over the tables. But the mood among the clientele was far from friendly. If anything, the conversation and the body language bristled with righteous anger – or at best sadness;

one could tell what was being said even when the words were not used: 'the country is going to hell'.

I recalled, a bit too loudly I guess, the experience my wife and I had with the emotive 'power of darkness' while living in New York. It was July 2003 during that now infamous 'rippling power outage' that spread across much of Canada and north-east America. Our apartment, 29 floors up, overlooked the Con Edison power plant close to the East River. It was late afternoon and I was at my desk when an explosion shook our building; everything around me was plunged into silence, and then utter darkness when night came. First the electricity was gone, then the water stopped flowing because the pumps ceased functioning; soon we couldn't flush toilets. 29 floors up everything depended on electricity.

For 24 hours we climbed down and up a dark and narrow staircase, ferrying bottles of water to drink, brush teeth and flush toilets. In the shops we jostled with others for the disappearing supplies of water; we dodged the homicidal motorists who saw pedestrians as fair game, and watched them lean their heads out of their cars to cuss each other profanely as they battled for right of way at intersections because the traffic lights were not working. Afterwards, we learnt that 10 million people were similarly affected. In that Illovo restaurant, my description of Third World chaos in mighty New York was mostly greeted with silence, or with peremptory dismissal: this is systemic, not the same thing.

Yes, what was the point of that comparison? People don't suffer comparatively, they only suffer. Agreed. Except that all suffering has its context, and therein lies the answer to an appropriate response. I could have imposed on my friends another apocryphal anecdote. In 1993, as a visiting professor of literature at the New York City University's Harlem Campus, I taught creative writing to an adult class of mostly immigrant students. I was waxing lyrical about our unfolding miracle when a Brazilian student interrupted me: 'Professor, get real; your miracle will only take you to the threshold of the challenges we have been facing for decades.' I should have heeded her.

I could have repeated at the Illovo dinner how, often on my travels as a UN official, I had to cope with the challenges visitors to our country face. I have watched my luggage being 'walked away' at the airport in Quito, Ecuador, while I was held back behind a glass barrier by complicit customs officials; brushed my teeth with Coca Cola in a posh Bangkok hotel because of a water contamination scare; hopped over excrement-filled puddles in a 'township' overlooking Rio's famous Ipanema Beach. I could even add that my son Zachary, then 9 months old, endured with us many hours of icy solitude aboard a luxury train stranded between Milan and Geneva.

The point is that societal failures - economic, social, political - are cyclical and happen everywhere, all the time. Perhaps the difference in the way people cope is in part psychological. Americans reacted with both inner and outer fury when terrorists penetrated their super-secure borders and when their power management system failed to anticipate the enormous 2003 energy failure. This kind of thing just does not happen in the rich and mighty USA. Are we South Africans similarly 'spoilt', albeit for a different reason?

Did the 'perfect gift' of our political miracle - a peaceful transition away from the abyss of racial conflict, through a period of unprecedented macro prosperity, and the attainment of living standards at least for the growing middle class that still compares favourably with most developing countries and many developed countries - ill prepare us to respond to those inevitable, cyclical setbacks? Is that why we have moved so rapidly, within a short 14 years since 1994, from enervating euphoria to disabling despair?

I've lived abroad long enough, and travelled enough to know that we have - in South Africa - what business people call a 'going concern' and this is not a metaphor for leaving. But good things don't come as gifts. The time has come for all of us to leave our Illovo restaurant and other whinge retreats, roll up our sleeves, and get to work tackling the problems that face our country.

Perhaps it is time to re-energise or even reinvent those civil society organisations that helped us cope with and overcome the dysfunctional apartheid system. Let's recognise that government, everywhere in the world, is not the answer to all our problems, nor should we expect it to be. Outside of those five-year elections, we also have a continuous role to play.

Let's take, by way of comparison again, the United States: there are non-governmental and community organisations active in almost in every sphere of social endeavour, from health to education to saving energy and even the planet itself. Just ask the federal, state and local authorities that are relentlessly being lobbied on every issue imaginable. But the more progressive among these authorities will also admit that the really good NGOs aren't obsessively oppositional. They are always seeking and providing alternatives to state actions and policies that don't work.

So, if they can work at it, why can't we?

Achmat Dangor, Writer

Let's get positive

I saw this quote and it inspired me even more to delete the negative stuff I get and send out the positive stuff I get. My son came home from the UK after 2 years and he kept on saying – 'Mom we have the most beautiful country.'

Brick walls

Remember, the brick walls are there for a reason. The brick walls are not there to keep us out. The brick walls are there to give us a chance to show how badly we want something.

Randy Pausch

Let's get positive and show the world we can inspire people to love, to save and to grow in being a humble, funny, clean, great South Africa. If your department lacks leadership – show them how to do it – do not complain about it.

Alma Manders

Be the silver lining! (with thanks)

First of all, a very large thank you to Mr Knott-Craig for this letter - I received a copy while travelling overseas and it really was inspirational.

I am employed as a tour director in Europe, working for a renowned international touring company, and I spend nearly all of my time taking groups of foreigners through 35 plus countries, from France and Germany to Bosnia and Albania. Sadly, I constantly have to spend time defending my country to the many people that I meet who are fascinated to meet a South African. One of the first questions people ask (predictably) is whether or not I feel safe at home. I always reply that I feel safer in my hometown (Joburg) than I do on the streets of Paris and Rome, and as a proudly patriotic South African I endeavour to explain what a wonderful home South Africa can be. International media paints a very bleak picture of South Africa abroad, as do many ex-pats (a distressing number of whom are young and qualified).

Since my return to SA in March, I have noticed an all-pervading negativity in South Africa that I had never perceived before. Having not experienced the side-effects of the legendary 'load-shedding' (yet!), and having been overseas during the Polokwane convention and other such political debacles,

I did not foresee this negative attitude when I returned. My immediate reaction to any negative comment has always been to disregard it and instead focus on the positives, but on this visit I have taken a far quieter, observatory role. With the worldliness that travel brings, and the experiences that I have had in some of the world's richest, poorest, and most interesting countries, I do definitely have a new perspective on the South African situation.

I can see now that there are many issues that need to be tackled in our country, and many of these rightly make us nervous. However, I do not believe that any of us can predict the future (esteemed analysts aside), and the (ever-increasing) doomsayers who keep commenting that 'this country has gone to the dogs' are some of the very people whose attitude and commitment to South Africa could change the country's future. Instead, too many have taken the victim route and are looking for someone to take out their fears on. I know that far too many people have fallen victim to the darker side of South Africa, and that there are numerous problems that our new democracy is facing at present, but I do believe that, as Mr Knott-Craig says, there is indeed a silver lining in every cloud. All we need to do now is embrace the positives, work hard at destroying the negatives, and most of all, be constructive.

I can see now with renewed clarity how much we have to offer and the unlimited potential of this country! If everyone who was enlightened by this wonderful letter makes an effort to pay it forward: sponsor a homeless child for a year, donate books and blankets, and say a good word about our country, we will become the silver lining in our current cloud!

KLH

The reward of risk

I recognise that living in South Africa involves great risk on many levels, even risk to our survival. I recognise that living in South Africa involves confronting our own prejudices and fears on a daily basis, as we live right next door to them. I recognise that our infrastructure, services, political and moral leadership (and national soccer team) could all do with a kick up the arse sometimes.

Our closest friends in Joburg were shot in their beds three weeks ago, so I know intimately the sadness and the loss that can be part of living in this country. While I don't consider myself loyal to South Africa, nor to any other place for that matter, I also recognise that: engaging with risk, confronting my prejudices, enlarging my world view,

learning from diversity, having my creativity
stretched, contributing to miracles, making
a difference and feeling the sun on my back
are very wonderful parts of being human to
me. Thank you, South Africa, for allowing me
that. Look forward not backwards.

Angela Deutschmann

Perspective

What a great letter! I love this place. I
don't deny there are some terrifying things
happening, but complaining about it and getting
caught up in hysteria certainly doesn't help.
Sometimes appreciating the small things is all
that counts. There are a million opportunities
here - so much work to be done, so many minds
to change, so many points to prove and so many
hurdles to leap over ... I'm here to stay and
fight my fights - what kind of person would I
be if I bailed, knowing I could do some good?
SA rocks!

Jacky

The grass ain't greener

I just want to say we have one of the most
beautiful countries in the world, and the grass

ain't greener on the other side. I know of a
few people that have left our country and want
to come back (but can't face their friends).
So what does that say to us? Be grateful and
look after yourself and talk to your neighbour
and make more friends.

Isabel du Plessis

How are you, South Africa?

It was a time when it was hard to be positive.
When it seemed that fate, criminals and the
South African government were conspiring to
rub salt in the wounds. When three friends had
been shot dead in the space of a year. When
Eskom had suddenly woken from a decade-long
slumber to discover it couldn't deliver power
to the people of South Africa.

It was especially hard to be positive when
friends and acquaintances began making plans
to depart for less-blighted landscapes. It was
torture to be positive when friends who had
already left the country wrote to say 'I told
you so' – not in triumphal tones, but in sad
affirmation that they had 'escaped' in time.

But it wasn't easy to be negative, either.
I didn't want to believe that we should simply
give up on this beautiful country for which so
many of us had sacrificed so much. I couldn't
accept that the South Africa that was so

deeply ingrained in my soul could so easily be dismantled by murderers and bureaucrats.

As they have it in works of inspirational fact and fiction, this character needed a sign.

And then someone greeted me. It was an unremarkable greeting from a cashier in an unmemorable store in a faceless mall, and it was a greeting with no particular significance: 'How are you?' she asked. 'Good thank you, and you?' I replied. 'Fine thank you, and thank you for asking,' she responded.

I would have thought no more of it, but suddenly realised she was smiling as she rang up the items. A new store policy? I glanced across at the other cashiers. It was business as usual: none of them were smiling.

It was hardly the first time I had noticed that effect. But until that moment I had always taken for granted the ease with which people in South Africa greeted each other. I had unconsciously come to accept the fact that, if you ask total strangers how they are – whether encountering them in an elevator in a corporate palace, whether they are knocking on your door to sell a broom, or whether they are on the other end of a cash register – these South Africans will treat you as a human being rather than as a blur in the passing picture of faceless humanity.

So while it wasn't the first time I had experienced a warm response to a simple greeting of a complete stranger, it came in the days after another friend had been murdered, and I was floundering for a sign that the end was not nigh.

The sign was, in reality, the coalescing of many vague memories and encounters. It had been there all along.

For the next few days, I chose not to wait for the greeting, as I had tended to in the past. Instead, I asked that exquisitely simple question of every stranger with whom I interacted – in stores, parking garages, security entrances, offices, restaurants and filling stations: 'How are you?'

The response was astonishing. Without exception, every one of the 'strangers' I addressed broke into a smile, often starting up a conversation about the weather, sometimes about my car, even about the shirt I was wearing, or perhaps about the state of South African sport.

If I was distracted and forgot to ask the question, it would usually be asked of me. When I responded in kind, what would often have been an irritable encounter became an affirmation of the warmth lurking beneath the South African surface.

In the many countries to which privileged South Africans are fleeing, there is no tradition of such basic interaction between strangers, and its absence will probably not even be noticed. But a rich undercurrent in the lives of these nomads will disappear, and they won't even know it.

Only three words, but they carry with them the hope of a wonderful country.

Arthur Goldstuck, writer

If we lighten up, we can survive this crisis

When Chris Hani was assassinated, South Africa teetered on the brink of civil war.

When the negotiations in the 1990s were threatened by third force violence and intransigence, we teetered again.

When we formed those long queues to vote in 1994, the predicted chaos did not happen.

What did South Africans do at those critical junctures?

They listened, asked questions, respected other opinions, put aside egos, made decisions and stuck to them.

And they had goodwill. They thought perhaps about South Africa first rather than themselves.

If our leaders in government, in industry, in Eskom, in our homes, you and me, dig deep and emulate the 'impossible' optimism of the early 1990s we can survive this (electricity) crisis and emerge a stronger, wiser, more mature people.

Cynicism is the enemy of change. Hope and

goodwill are the tools for positive change. And let's lighten up – that'll help.

Bearnard O'Riain, Johannesburg

Why I love this country

One can do the standard white cliche's ... sunny skies, rugby, *boerewors* and Kruger Park, etc, but you really have to think deeper than that to negate the armed heists, rape, murder and general *kak* of Eskom, home affairs and Bafana Bafana ... and the South African rugby and cricket authorities. I remember a time when I bemoaned the fact that I was an economic prisoner in my own country, I couldn't afford to leave and go to Oz, but in all honesty I never wanted to. Funny thing though, when my kids brought the subject up, I must admit, I told them to go. Mixed emotions I guess. White or black, you always want the best for your kids and given the current stats here, is there a great future for them?

Then I got to thinking, probably rather selfishly, that this would mean that I would get old alone. A visit twice a year, if I could afford it. Blotchy conversations on Skype and please God my health doesn't go, otherwise they get the dreaded SMS from my mates at the pub: 'Right said Fred. Your Dad's dead. Nuff said!' Selfish in other ways as well, I must confess. I was thinking about MY kids. They qualify, you see, ... they can get the points and pass the language test, they have skills that make them attractive to the Aussie employment market.

My wife then, inadvertently, provided me with a clue to the answer. On a trip to Jozi, she had dealings with a car guard who thanked her in French. Being the curious conversational type she asked him where he was from. Turns out he's from the Congo and he's a professor of history but with all the *kak* up there the varsity is shut and he can't get a job. Him and a few mates take a small stroll to Jozi, find a spot to squat and do what they can for a crust. Here's the point of the story: Every month they pool their money and take it in turns to send cash home. Mainly to feed the family, but they also put aside a bit for when things come right up there and they can go back. They believe in their country even though right now it's a hellhole! They love the place ...

Many thousands of Zimbos working all over the world remit money every month to create a future for their families left behind. When Bob goes they will return. Their combined remittance is bigger than the foreign aid donations. They do it because they love their country!

South Africa is way ahead of those two places and I have to believe that there is just so much to love about this country. There are also millions like you and me who really don't want live anywhere else. We have to become the engine for positive change – governments and fancy constitutions cannot be relied upon to be this engine.

We, as individuals, constantly ask the question: What do I want from this country? Let's change the question and ask: What does this country want from me?

Think on this for a while, friend of mine. Make a list of the things you, just you, my old mate, could do to make things just a little better. Start small . . . like turn off a light when it's not needed. Take a minute to pick up some litter and put it in a bin. Think about the skills you have and teach them to one other person who doesn't have them. You can bet your last rand they will teach that skill to someone else – that's how Granny's recipes and Granddad's remedy got into your head. Ask around, see what your neighbour needs, maybe he's a plumber who could train others and could do it if you find a mate of yours to give his wife a lift to work on Saturdays. Let's find out how many reservists our local police station needs to do the admin that keeps a cop off the beat.

We are used to pyramid selling in this country. Let's sell our service to our country for free. You find one person who commits to you, to help this cause, he finds one, who in turn finds one, who finds another. I will do the same. In a few weeks we will have a platoon, in months, an army that can provide salvation.

There is no doubt that this country is worth loving. Our own citizens fought each other, up until recently, for the right to live in peace and harmony as equals in this wonderful land. The bottom line is that we have to stop seeing each other as groupings and see each other as South Africans ... and each of us needs to find answers to the question: what does my country need from me?

It needs us to serve its needs before our own. It needs us to talk to each other rather than tell each other. Let's you and me start. Small steps ... one at a time ... I'll buy you lunch when we're finished.

Hamba kahle

Patrick Smythe

The ups

We have the best weather. I have visited 18 countries so far and we are the best. We have one of the biggest biodiversities in the world and the most diverse mix of cultures. This country is vibey and it buzzes. Not like Australia, which is like a giant old-age home. South Africa rocks – where else can you do all your shopping at the robots?

Daryl Lawrence, Johannesburg

Think yellow!

Think yellow - the colour of the sun, of light and laughter, warmth and comfort, of mealies and sunflowers; the colour of energy and inspiration. We need to be inspired to speak out about all the good things we have in abundance in this country. Sure, South Africa's not perfect and the crime is really scary - but it is still a great place to grow old in.

Shelagh Stow

Dreary Switzerland

I was delighted to receive your positive message this morning. I am sitting here in Bern, having just taken early retirement from my interesting job of 16 years as I am coming home to South Africa for good.

I left Joburg 30 years ago because of apartheid and have lived in Leeds, Harare and then Bern, and I have always missed Joburg. For the last five years I have come home to Joburg every year to complete the supervised practical training with the Institute of Traumatology. This training involved me working intensively with Victim Support Units of three SAPS stations, going out with the police to serious situations and sometimes working with the emergency services. This was gruelling for an old duck in her late 50s, but I did it and qualified in 2006 so that I could come home and do something meaningful with my life.

I think the most important aspect for me was the development of a really deep and passionate love of my city - especially living in my flat in Yeoville and watching the area go down and now come up. I love the community with its multi-African culture and I can see the whole of the north of the metropolis from my front balcony and a lot of the city from the kitchen window. My husband and I like to sit on our balcony with a glass of wine as the sun sets with the slowly changing light over the urban forest toward the Magaliesberg. By the second glass the scene is a mass of blinking lights with Ponte and the Post Office Tower shining into the kitchen window. We will buy a small house with a little garden, but that view will be a hard act to follow and I am keeping that flat.

I have spent time in many of Europe's finest cities and in Switzerland we live in this uniquely preserved 800-year-old city which nestles on a half peninsula into the beautiful Aare River. It is a World Heritage site and the panoramic views of the mighty Alps are spectacular on a clear day. It is safe and calm and slow moving and I can walk everywhere I need to go and never drive. Sounds like paradise I know, but it just does not move me to those magic warm all-over sensations I get in Joburg. I need the buzz and the unpredictability, the noise, the crazy traffic, the incredible creativity abounding in music, literature and theatre. I miss the long hot walks in the Botanical Gardens and my weekly stroll right through various parts of the now very African city.

Finally I have to say there is a feeling in the Joburg which I have never encountered anywhere else and there is humour and laughter in abundance too - I laugh and talk more there than I have anywhere else.

Elaine Kramers, Bern, Switzerland

No ... I'm staying

Never before have I found myself in the company of such 'gloom'. It seems that a day cannot pass without someone asking me if I'm considering leaving! My answer is always the same, as it was when I wrote this for a newsletter six years ago:

Recently, I did a strange thing. I moved to Gauteng; I moved from Cape Town, from an ideal location overlooking the Atlantic and within shouting distance of white sands and majestic mountains. The seed was originally sown in my reluctant mind by enticing offers of money, position and career growth, but as the roots started to force their way down into my heart and soul, I began to realise that my love for this country was not borne out of white beaches and blue seas, but from those trips as a little girl to a great uncle's farm along the banks of the Crocodile River with my grandmother. I recall the space, lots and lots of it. The sky seemed so enveloping and huge and clear and those morning visits to the little trading store along the dusty road, vibrant with little yellow chicks, filled the memory with a kaleidoscope of possibilities.

So it was with fists full of anticipation and excitement that I made my move to the pulsing heart of our country with my husband and little child; she too deserved to feel the rhythm and energy of South Africa.

Now, only two months later, when people ask me whether I've managed to settle down (with a frown of pity on their faces), I find myself unable to answer immediately, because the strange thing is that it feels like I've come home. The home from which all else in the country feeds. I sometimes imagine the energy spreading like a spiderweb of veins to reach the jagged borders that surround us. It hums. I will probably end up back in Cape Town one day but it will always be with knowing where I really come from and why I returned from opportunities elsewhere in the world. It will be with a bursting heart for the spirit and generosity and colours of Africa and with an open mind to see and accept all things in relation to the vastness and total offering of this land of ours.

Dale Knowles-Gaylard, Johannesburg

South Africa will never leave you

In 1988 we went to live in the United States. I had finally given up hope that apartheid would ever relinquish its death grip on the country and its people, and I wanted my children to be raised without the indelible infection of racial prejudice that had contaminated the great majority of white families.

Yet after 14 years in America, my husband and I made the difficult decision to come home. We left two of our three children behind. They had grown up as we had planned and become American adults. But my husband and I had not grown with them. Instead, as the years went by, our African soulscape – an interior landscape that no other land can replace – grew ever more powerful. It came to us that we did not want to grow older in a country that, despite the long years, remained foreign to us in so many ways.

We have been back in South Africa since 2002, and people still ask why we left 'Paradise

California' for a country plagued by violent crime, poverty, corruption and unemployment. My husband tells them it's because we've been; we know what it's like to live in another country and we've made our choice, and if you're still here, he adds, so have you.

Living away from home is an experience unlike any other. It brings out both the best and the worst in people. Our experience prompts me to persuade would-be runaways that South Africa offers its people the greatest of all opportunities: to abandon the herd psychology of pessimism and fear and instead welcome the challenges of working together; the nation-building that promises to make this country even more of what it has always been: a place of miracles.

I have observed that the people who are most fearful and negative are those who live on the fat of the land, whose homes and security systems ensure that they are less likely to be exposed to the evils of poverty and crime that routinely make victims out of township and shack dwellers, and always have. These privileged people grumble that they have the most to lose. Well, losing your country is one of the greatest losses in this life. We learned in America that another country presents a different set of challenges, but problems are multiplying everywhere, no matter where you choose to live. And that's the nub of it: uprooting yourself in hope of a better, safer life is merely that: a hope. In reality it is simply a matter of personal choice where you decide to spend the only thing in this world that you truly own: your short life.

For all its problems, South Africa is one of the most diverse and exciting places in the world to live. We live more fully, more gratefully now that we ever did, at home among our people and our city of mountains and oceans.

Leave this country if you will, but from long experience I can promise it will never leave you.

Rosemund Handler, writer

Are we staying?

My whole family is still in South Africa. We have invested everything we have here in property and business. To us the answer is very simple, we are not going anywhere. And there are literally millions and millions of South Africans whose whole lives are so entrenched in this country. We simply have to get through this difficult period and prosper again. I get the idea a lot of highly trained people and especially whites are so afraid of being 'left behind'. But they must just relax, there is enough capital in this country to keep drawing intellectuals - and the world is such an open market that remuneration packages will even out the shortages, whether it is in SA or in the Europe.

Look at country like India. Although there is still a lot of poverty, the country now has a booming middle class and some of the world's most high-tech innovations come from there. But this wasn't always the case and until about a decade ago, nobody really took India seriously. One of the reasons stated for the turnaround in India is because thousands of members of the Indian diaspora worldwide starting ploughing back into their country of origin. Lots of them returned with capital and vast experience. I firmly believe that the diaspora of South Africans is not just doom and gloom. Many of them will return and many of them will make a positive difference. We just need a positive vibe among investors about South Africa for a few years and progress in areas like crime reduction, and before we know it, South Africa will bloom like never before.

Capital always flows towards places with the best return to risk ratio. I don't think the 'risks' in the SA economy are really that great and together with the commodity boom, which seems likely to continue for a few more years, the return in the South African economy could be very high. Therefore capital will not run away. Yes, there might be individuals and even a handful of companies who will leave the country and take money out, but the real capital from big corporates should keep on coming.

There are obviously also a lot of emotional reasons why I want to stay and fight for my country.

Gerhard van Deventer

A better South Africa

Thank you for the initiative that has been taken by Alan Knott-Craig. If possible, during the busy-ness of his day, I hope he is being made aware of how many of his fellow South Africans also believe that South Africa is an amazing country to be privileged to live in.

I was born in the UK, married a South African and have lived in this beautiful country since 1970. I became a South African citizen in 1990. Yes I do have an escape route, back to the UK, but why would any one want to live in the UK again?

Living in SA is not just about the wide open spaces, the smell of the bush, the blending of different cultures, it is also about challenge and we as South Africans have to rise to this challenge.

We are all aware of the negatives facing this country so I wont bother to list them

here, however, let us all move forward to
embrace the future. Above all, please don't let
us become a nation of whiners, like the Poms,
let us all in some small way try to be more
proactive and to be accepting of our fellow
South Africans, despite colour or creed.

Penny Cole

Land of opportunity and success

I left South Africa about 4 years ago, very
disillusioned by the crime and the downward
economic spiral. I was hijacked 3 times in the
period of a year and was then told that BEE
would affect my position within the company
that I was working for. With all of the above
in mind I decided enough was enough.

I moved over to the UK with my wife and
landed probably one of the best jobs of my life.
Together my wife and I earned the equivalent
of the payout of the lottery in South Africa
with our yearly salaries. We moved to a small
community in Surrey and a short while later
decided to start a family.

I never returned to South Africa during
this period as I had left some very deep scars
behind and did not want to reopen any of the
memories. In year three of my employment at
the company I stumbled upon an opportunity of
a lifetime. The company was in the process of

outsourcing to a number of countries, but was constantly beaten back when it came to the quality of English. I literally travelled the planet from Barbados, Mauritius, Philippines, Czech Republic and Grenada to many others. I just could not find anyone who could provide the level of English required.

I thought long and hard about South Africa and decided to pitch the concept to the board of directors at the company. They all had a good laugh and made reference to the extreme circumstances that I had experienced while living here. The proposal was declined, much to my dismay. I went home to my then 7 month pregnant wife and told her I was going to resign my position with the company and return to South Africa for a short period of time to 'test the waters'.

Four months down the line, after the birth of my first child and many hours of flying between the UK and South Africa, I brought both my child and wife out to South Africa. I started a company where I piloted a test centre in Johannesburg for the company I had worked for in the UK. This company is now my primary client.

I am still not totally at ease with the country and the current state of crime and economic instability, but I am glad to return to my country of birth and help build it and try and to put it back to the top where it should be.

I hope this story shows people that South Africa is the land of opportunity and success, let's hope that the government of the day can keep this country on the straight and narrow and get it moving in the right direction.

Gerald G Groenewald

Positive thoughts

South Africa's economy has been monitored by Trevor Manuel and Tito Mboweni and must be the envy of the Americans right now, as their economy is facing recession. Our National Credit Act and the steps taken to contain consumer debt have resulted in our own economy now being stronger than that of the USA.

Where in the world could you walk down the street and be greeted and smiled at by most passers-by? Here in South Africa I am asked how I am, I am greeted cheerfully as 'Gogo' and I am made to feel good when I have my daily walk in my suburb.

Keep up the good work with positive thoughts - we need them more than ever with so many people spreading negativity as they criticise the power supply, the crime, the state of the roads, etc. Some people seem to vie with one another to tell the worst negative stories and we have to do our best to counteract them!

Kit Bradford

The accidental expat

We decided to return to South Africa after nine years abroad - two years in the UK consulting and seven years in Sydney. One Christmas in London was enough to cure us of the dream and romance of a white Christmas, give us the sun and the beach any day. So the chance to head Down Under was opportune, and we headed off to help start up Virgin Mobile in Sydney.

After seven years in Sydney we were well settled, had made a new group of friends, had got ourselves involved in kids and sporting pursuits, and had found our niche, both socially and in business - to the extent that my consultancy was running at full capacity and I had even been voted one of the top 10 marketing personalities in Australia by *B&T Magazine*. So coming back was not a decision based on a lack of opportunity or success in Australia.

I guess that's why it may seem a bit strange to some people. So I thought I would try to give some insight into why we have moved, as well as my perceptions of Australian life - particularly with the current 'grass is greener' mentality and discussions again doing the rounds in South Africa.

The reasons to come back are simple - our family are still in South Africa (in the Eastern Cape), and we wanted to spend with them and let our kids spend quality time with their grandparents. We wanted to be part of an extended family.

We also wanted to see what we could do to help get this great country running at its true potential. That may sound like opportunistic armchair liberal crap, but being away gives you a clearer perspective on the country, the opportunities we were afforded and a sense of obligation to help.

What this will result in, in terms of actual input or output, is anyone's guess - but writing this article is a start if it gives a different perspective to those wishing to pack it in.

We didn't make a list of pros and cons about moving, but we spent a year talking about it before making a decision. I also made a trip out here to see what opportunities there would be for me to start a marketing consultancy here - particularly as we did not want to move back to Joburg. The trip was more encouraging and positive than I could have hoped for, with everyone I met exceptionally upbeat about not only the level of opportunities, but also the potential and future of the country. That ticked a big box - yes, we would probably be able to earn a decent living. So we packed up and moved back - the accidental expats returned.

And what about Australia? Australia is a reasonably easy transition for South Africans wishing to emigrate. In a lot of respects it is similar to SA - they love sport, they have an outdoors lifestyle and culturally, they tend to have some similar ideas. It has low rates of crime, lower rates of interest, social and economic structures that work and very low levels of unemployment which result in a high demand for skills. It is a country which is easy to live in, with great beaches and recreation facilities, good schools and on the whole very sociable people. It is a country where you can live comfortably in the thick middle class, but where it is exceedingly difficult to get ahead. Australia is a very socialist country, where the status quo is praised, middle-class equality is encouraged, and tall poppies are cut down as fast as they arise. You should not expect praise or support for successful entrepreneurial ventures. If your ambition is to live a comfortable life of relative success and anonymity it might just be the ideal destination.

If however, you do not want to be overregulated and conformist, and want to get out there and set the world alight by challenging the status quo, you will find it frustrating and confining. This is not just due to the regulations, but also due to the mentality of the majority of the population - amazingly, all those out-there, go-getter Aussies you meet while backpacking, become conformist, consensus-driven wage slaves when they get home. (I know that is a massive generalisation, but it is also my very strong observation.) Decisions are deferred to the committee and commitment is avoided, particularly if the decision goes against the norm.

What the Australians have done exceptionally well is to market themselves, internally and externally. I am not talking specifically about a tourism campaign or any specific piece of communication, but rather about the overall communications which have resulted in a huge sense of national pride and a global perception of Australia being the relocation destination of choice. They are widely thought of as the land of opportunity, and you only have to look at how many South Africans have headed there to see how successful it has been.

Australians have, for the last 20-odd years, been targeted by campaigns which build this sense of national pride - where FMCG products are stamped with the 'Australian Owned/Australian Made' stamp to guarantee that profits and jobs are staying in the country. This led to changed consumer behaviour, where marginal local brands suddenly became market leaders by being local. Their sports teams are given heroes' welcomes and are actively marketed and involved in the community. They spend a small fortune on television advertising and events to reinforce this message and take it to the rest of the world. They have actively controlled their messaging globally rather than rely on the media to do the job for them.

This is a lesson which South Africa needs to learn. We need to actively engage the necessary partners and resources to manage our image and messages to the world. For too long we have let the world's media control what is said and heard about South Africa rather than have a strategic campaign to build the country's positives.

Yes, we have our problems, and yes some of the media is not pretty, but why are we not at least delivering the positives to balance the negative press? We have just won the rugby World Cup, but three months later, what has been done to leverage this? I don't see anything - even our internal messages and media are dominated by Eskom, crime, rates rises and the like - where are the images and stories that make me proudly South African? I am not advocating that we bury our heads in the sand, but if we don't expose and celebrate the positive, how can we hope to have any positive coverage abroad?

I have seen the Proudly South African stickers on cars, but what else is being done? And more importantly, how are we making sure that it works? If the current wave of sentiment is any indicator, I would say it is not working. There seem to be a lot of people who are seriously considering 'packing for Perth', and that does not sound like a successful campaign.

Eskom seems to be the main reason - we can't supply electricity, the water system is collapsing, we are going to hell in a handbasket, SA is the next Zimbabwe... did I miss any?

These are all problems we can overcome. We survived the transition from apartheid to a true democracy without a civil war ... surely this is just a speed bump in our road to progress? Maybe if we all did our bit instead of bitching and moaning we might achieve a fast, effective solution ... it's worth a shot.

So, why did we come home? Well, first of all it is home, and always will be. We are fiercely proud South Africans and to live somewhere else will always be a compromise. This country is part of our DNA and we want to help it get stronger and live up to its potential. There is massive opportunity here for anyone wanting to grab it and just go for it. And, I want to live surrounded by the family and friends we love. Surely that should be enough reason for anyone.

Rich Field

A calm centre

We are living in world where changes are happening all around us. It is a time where people in general are feeling insecure and bewildered as to where to go and what steps to take to feel safer and more secure. In South Africa we are faced with negative press and negative conversation at the dinner table, sport fields or at work.

The consolation to all of this is that it does not matter which country you are living in, or how wealthy or poor you may be. The conversations you are hearing at home in South Africa are similar to those in other countries. In some cases the conversations elsewhere are far more daunting! The most important issue here is to try keep your centre calm while the tornado of life and the world creates havoc around you. To keep yourself centred in the belief that you are doing all that you can to be a wiser, more enlightened individual who is making a positive impact on the world in which you live.

We are truly the centre of our world and if you apply yourself in a positive way with positive actions you can only reap positive energy around you. Yes, we are scared at times and find ourselves faced with our fears - this is the challenge of being human. The challenge of growing into what you can truly be. South Africa has faced battles that many countries have not had the courage to face - we have risen above and stood for the miracle of a country which has never been drowned in anarchy no matter our history or challenges. We have the most diverse environment with the magic of our people that we can be so proud of.

I am a proud South African. I will always carry with me an upbringing and sense of being that I can only thank my country and fellow South Africans for.

Kim Feinberg, The Tomorrow Trust

For my children

If you read the newspapers every morning, as I do, you may be struck by how miserable we all are. If police catch a gang of cash-in-transit heist robbers, they are accused of excessive force. If a crime goes unresolved, the self-same police are accused of ineptitude. If you go online to the British or American newspapers you will find the same thing. The world has never seemed more miserable or afraid than it is now. But is that true? Are we really in a worse place than ever before? Go back 30 or 40 years, front-page news included terror stories about the next ice age, nuclear war, the death of the nuclear family. There's never been a time when we haven't been facing some kind of life-threatening or lifestyle-threatening crisis. Fear has become part of our DNA. With reason? Maybe. But it's not a legacy I want to hand down to my children.

I want them to grow up golden in the sun that shines all year round, almost every day. I want them to swim in the warm seas off the north

WORLD CUP 2010

YEBO!

Inside your World Cup paper

Here we snatched the votes from our rivals

PLUS
Brenda's last crack binge

2005

Sunday Times

Asked to resign, embattled deputy tells the President's messengers to get lost

Fire me, Zuma dares Mbeki

1994 **Sunday Times**

R500 000

Hospitals flooded by AIDS patients

1991

The fury that left three dead as AWB battled with police

Sunday Times

OPEN WAR

2006

The Star
BUSINESS REPORT
MAY 02 2006

GOLD TO BREACH $800 MARK

1996

Sunday Times

A nation of champions
Bafana Bafana make it a soccer, rugby and cricket triple

100 YEARS **Sunday Time**

SA's millionaire boom
In just one year, BEE deals help propel a 'phenomenal' people into the 43 000-strong ranks of the seriously

and south KwaZulu-Natal coastline. I want to take them on hikes through the Drakensberg and teach them to braai. My head's not in the sand about the problems we face, but there are opportunities for learning and growth here as well. My kids will grow up able to protect themselves from UV rays by wearing the sunscreen we never did, from living on landfill by learning to recycle. They will use electricity sensibly and value the land around them. The next generation is the one that will change the world, I am sure of it. Nobel Prize winner Rabindranath Tagore said: 'Every child comes with the message that God is not yet discouraged of man.' If the all-seeing, all-knowing eternal power has faith in us, then who are we to drown our hopes and dreams in newspaper headlines?

Sam Cowen, 94.7 Highveld Stereo

Make a difference

A country is defined by its people. No person is perfect and no country will ever be perfect. But every South African citizen can make a difference. Each of us can choose whether we want the difference we make to have either a positive or negative impact. Building a healthy, vibrant nation is a journey. It requires every citizen to actively participate in the building process. It requires a government committed to social and economic development. And it requires a belief in and realisation of the greatness that defines South Africa.

Andile Ngcaba, Chairman, Didata

Blackouts = time with my children

Thank you Eskom for the blackouts, because now I have to sit with my children and play games with them instead of them being glued to the television. Blackouts make bath time fun as we fill the bathroom with candles and add more bubble bath.

Thank you Eskom as blackouts mean I can't cook a big meal ... so I get to spend even more time with my children and I get them involved in making the sandwiches etc in the kitchen. And watch out for the baby boom in less than 9 months time because now I have no TV to distract me from giving my husband a little more affection!

Thank you Eskom for making us more aware of the energy crisis and making us use energy saving devices. Thank you Eskom. There's always a silver lining ... even though I can't see it because the street lights are out!

Angela Plows

Home

Today I held the future of South Africa in my arms. She was 8 months old and had one of the loveliest smiles I'd ever seen. We were at the local Checkers store waiting for our family members to complete the monthly grocery shopping and to pass the time her mother and I exchanged stories about everyday life in SA - electricity cuts, the increase in crime, but then we started to share the really important stuff - what really mattered most - her dreams for her daughter to be well educated, her love for her son and her husband. And I was able to share the joy of recently celebrating my parents' 40th wedding anniversary, of spending time with loved ones over the past long weekend, of the Stormers winning abroad ... the list goes on.

For as fashionable as it may be to rant and rave about the negatives, the postives far outweigh them! This conversation with my neighbour, my fellow South African, reminded me of why we are such a great nation because this is home, our home, everyone's home and as the old adage states, if home is where the heart is - then my home is definitely with my people, right here, in South Africa!

Anine Pheiffer

Tomorrow

There is a saying that goes 'Africa's soul is red because of all the blood that has been spilt on it.' The irony is that once you have lived on that soul, and worked it, it pulls into your veins and beats in your heart, once this has happened the country will never leave you and you can never leave the country - no matter where you live.

Now is the time for each South African, abroad or in the country, to believe in this amazing country. Put your faith in the people, the creative South Africans, who never take no for an answer. The people find new ways to make old things work. People who smile and talk and care, people who sell papers at traffic lights and always have time for a joke while you scramble for that R5. The fruit seller who works long hours in the sun but still negotiates the price of the juicy box of litchis with a smile. The taxi driver that cuts across three lanes to pick up the finger pointing lady next to the slow lane.

South Africa pulses with a rhythm that can only be heard if you belong to her. A never-ending beat that pulses through our veins like the red soul we work, walk and live on. It is a country as unique as her people and so misunderstood by anybody outside her borders.

Now is the time for each South African to

believe in who we are, what we have created and what we are capable of still achieving. Don't let the world tell us who we are and what we should think of our country. Let's focus on tomorrow and the opportunity that today brings. Every obstacle is a growing pain and every challenge an opportunity,

Yolanda Uys

Abundant colours

For an artist, it is a county filled with vibrant colours - each canvas challenging and different.

Everything that combines the diversity that is part of this beautiful South Africa.

Just so for a writer it is the description of the humour of the people of South Africa.

It is the blending of the various talents of those who live in this most unusual country.

For the actor it is a challenging role to portray the characters that make up this unique country. A country that we love, but a country that needs to be shown the love toward each other - each and every South African who abides in this land.

So what am I going to do about it?

Victoria Preece

Overcome

At first I was struck with negativity after hearing of the major power failures in Gauteng (which I did not experience since I live in the country). I started to panic when I heard how certain white reporters where treated at a Press conference. What am I going to do? I have three children in school and I cannot imagine immigrating to another country. South Africa is all I know. And then it struck me. What am I going to do about it? I can sit and bite my nails or I can find an intelligent way to overcome my fears. I might need to change my ways a bit, but I can overcome anything that comes my way. It is an attitude change. Maybe the electricity cuts are what we needed to start saving and looking for better and healthier alternatives. High crime forces us the make friends with neighbours so that we can look out for each other. South Africans are creative and intelligent, we have proven it many times, it is high time we start using it for our greater good.

Hestie Coetzee

Sustainability

I would like to thank Eskom - their load shedding debacle has encouraged us to become more self sustained. We have converted to solar geysers, we are looking at solar/wind generators for the whole house - this is first world stuff that most countries only happen apon after years and years of development! South Africans have a chance to be earth wise and work on their carbon foot prints while we all sit in the dark!

Thanks Eskom for all the Earth Hour practice. The big question - will South Africans willingly switch off their lights for an hour at 8pm on the 29th of March? If Eskom doesn't, we certainly will.

Carrie Cleminson, Johannesburg

Queueing

I'll tell you a thing we do really well in South Africa and that's queue! Orderly, no pushing, all repel queue jumpers but in a polite fashion, Usually someone (me) is chatting to strangers - we greet one another- we pass comments. In short we behave well regardless of the ethnic, gender, age mix. The power to make tomorrow the best.

Paddy Smith

God's power

Today I discovered that tomorrow is what you make of it today. Tomorrow is today's thoughts manifested. Position your mind properly and think straight, your tomorrow becomes obviously the best.

Sulaiman Maeresera

Pressure for the good

Recent developments in the country have led to a new wave of negativism and talk of the great Australian exodus is once again rife. As a holder of permanent residency in Australia and with two sons in that country I suggest that it is not yet time to panic. The green haze is not greener pastures it is only a shimmer of envy as that country offers no more than we have here. The problem with very stable societies like Australia is they don't have reckless courage, so exposure to the real world is slow and frustrating.

It is not time to become overly pessimistic. South Africans are tough and we have not yet risen to the bait thrown down by corrupt cops, government officials, rampant crime or the power blackouts. The reason for our tendency to whine and not rise up to the challenge is because we are not yet really under pressure.

It is difficult to become revolutionary when the weather is good, the economy is still improving (relative to the old days) and relationships between the races improve daily. Relationships can't be judged on the fury created by taxi drivers, it must be judged on the day-to-day interaction that we enjoy with the diverse people of this country.

Eskom has actually done us a great service: the shopping centres that I build find that by rotating air conditioning around the centres they can save 30% of their power consumption and the temperature impact is minor. Data centres are redesigned to consume only 50% of previous demand simply through the creativity of forced pressure. South Africa must and will rise to the challenge of Eskom because it is good for our region.

Lastly, don't try to change the whole of South Africa in one go and on your own. Let's change one person at a time.

L. Stapelberg, Pretoria

Remember when ...

When the big picture starts getting blurred by life's smaller irritants, it helps, probably when contemplating the affairs of countries too, to refocus. In the case of a young democracy like South Africa it means also casting a mind back. For me this entails recalling that memorable Friday of February 2, 1990 when so much changed.

I was sitting in my office at the Cape Argus newspaper in Cape Town, vaguely aware that the familiar chants from protest marches in the streets outside were changing to cheers. Soon I, too, learned that President F W de Klerk had, in his state-of-the-nation speech to parliament a short distance away, unbanned the ANC, PAC and SACP and opened the way for a negotiated settlement. I further remember how in the late afternoon of February 11 I wandered down from my house in Tamboerskloof to the Grand Parade, passing groups of quick-marching soldiers on the way and arriving just in time to see Nelson Mandela, after 27 years in jail, step up a few metres from where I was positioned to address the masses.

There were hair-raising situations to come between those events and the time in 1994 when South Africans of all races stood in the same queue to vote for their chosen parties. Even afterwards there were dangerous moments. But I recall the slogans that had gone before that February of 1990, of total onslaught and liberation before education, and the gunfire in the streets and the palls of smoke rising over townships, and I remember the fears I, as others, suffered about the country going up in flames as outright civil war drew ever closer. For me, that was the month when panic ended.

Sure, memories do fade with time and it becomes harder to touch up the bigger canvas in the mind's eye, particularly when confronted by factors like violent crime and the heartbreak and suffering, not to forget the constant debilitating fear, it causes. And then, instead of resolute action, you find the depressing scenarios of the head of police and of a former deputy president, now with rekindled hopes of becoming president, facing criminal charges.

Sure, unemployment and poverty remain a deep worry, as do, among others, disease and HIV/Aids, the difficulties health services are having in coping with their commendably extended operations to try to cater for all, the irresolute manner in which the incendiary land-restitution question is being handled, the troubles too many schools are having in meeting the demands of a country wishing to offer all its children and education, and, of course, power cuts, although in this instance there is the consolation that rapid development is much to blame.

Granted, the bigger picture should not be used to shield such problems. But tilt it sufficiently to see behind these difficulties and there, in striking relief, will appear a constitution befitting a highly civilised society, a political system that encourages freedom of expression, and an economy whose danger is that of getting beyond itself. Educators and parents will see in classrooms and on school grounds a generation taking shape that is less plagued by the racial estrangement and prejudices and inequalities of those that had gone before. Older sports lovers might sometimes reflect momentarily on the gloom of international isolation once suffered when they see our young stars shine around the world. Some travellers may cast a mind back to when South Africa was called the polecat of the world when they see the congestion at Johannesburg's OR Tambo Airport, despite constant extensions, and when they notice people wearing weirdly coloured shirts and others wearing socks with open sandals, all speaking with foreign accents and many wielding cameras, coming and going from hotels and hostelries, and walking the streets or browsing through shops and curio markets even in places the tourist industry had formerly hardly heard of.

As a journalist now mainly writing about environmental matters, the bigger picture for me includes a country of astonishing natural beauty which was able to celebrate its release from international isolation by hosting the seminal World Summit on Sustainable Development, the World Parks Congress and the BirdLife International Congress in short succession, and which has emerged as an influential voice in the environmental forums of the world. It portrays a country which has grown its nature reserves, not shrunk and imperilled them as feared by many of the old establishment who could not see conservation fitting anywhere on the priority list of a new ruling class to whom parks would conceivably have further epitomised their former exclusion.

You see in legislation, though not always in deed, conservation joining with greater determination than ever in the age-old battle with development. You see national boundary fences, some reinforced with steel cables and electric wiring, coming down so that neighbouring countries' adjoining nature reserves can be opened to each other and animals and people can cross safely, also in places where bitter wars were until not too long ago still fought.

You look at all this and you think to yourself, how much there is to be grateful for.

Leon Marshall, writer

Where to from here?

You can find more positive South African stories on these websites:

- **www.sagoodnews.co.za** - South Africa, The Good News showcases the good stories.
- **www.homecomingrevolution.co.za** - Homecoming Revolution is dedicated to supporting South Africans returning from abroad.
- **www.sarocks.co.za** - South Africa Rocks is a blog developed as an antidote to depressing expat blogs.

If you want to get involved in making a positive contribution to South Africa, here are some ideas. We will be posting more ideas (and please send us yours) on our websites **www.penguinbooks.co.za** and **www.iburst.co.za**:

- **www.greatergoodsa.co.za** - gives lots of ideas on how to get involved (using time, money, or skills) with good causes in South Africa.

- **www.scsh.co.za** - The Stop Crime ... Say Hello website has some great ideas for getting involved in making South Africa a wonderful country.

And, as always, you can find the rest of the news in the media.

Let's hope we don't see another edition in five years entitled: *Panic!*